DATE DUE

AUG 0 8 2002	JAN 2 7 2003	JUN 0 3 2006
SEP 0 3 2002	JAN 1 0 2004	JUN 2 7 2006
OCT 2 2 2002	MAY 2 7 2004	AUG 1 4 2006
NOV 2 0 2002	NOV 2 9 2004	SEP 2 6 2006
DEC 1 6 2002	DEC 0 2 2004	
MAY 0 3 2003	FEB 2 2 2005	
JUL 0 8 2003	JUN 1 1 2005	OCT 2 8 2006
AUG 1 1 2003	AUG 3 1 2005	NOV 3 0 2006
NOV 2 0 2003	NOV 2 9 2005	JAN 2 7 2007
AUG 2 2 2005	MAR 0 4 2006	MAR 1 6 2007
	APR 1 9 2006	SEP 0 6 2007
DEC 2 6 2013		DEC 1 2 2007
JAN 2 7 2014	SEP 2 0 4	FEB 1 1 2008

this
·little·barron's·
book belongs to

....

....

First edition for the United States and Canada published 1999 by
Barron's Educational Series, Inc.

Copyright © Penny Dann 1998

First published in Great Britain by Orchard Books in 1998.

All inquiries should be addressed to:
Barron's Educational Series, Inc.
250 Wireless Boulevard, Hauppauge, New York 11788
http://www.barronseduc.com

Library of Congress Catalog Card No.: 98-74972
International Standard Book No. 0-7641-0869-7

Printed in Italy

Old MacDonald Had a Farm

Penny Dann

• little • barron's •

Old MacDonald had a farm, *E-I-E-I-O!*

And on that farm he had a dog, E-I-E-I-O!
With a **woof**, **woof**, here,
and a **woof**, **woof**, there,

here a **woof**, there a **woof**,
everywhere a **woof**, **woof**.

Old MacDonald had a farm, E-I-E-I-O!

And on that farm he had a tractor, E-I-E-I-O!
With a **chug**, **chug**, here,
and a **chug**, **chug**, there,

here a **chug**, there a **chug**,
everywhere a **chug**, **chug**.

Old MacDonald had a farm, E-I-E-I-O!

And on that farm he had some sheep, E-I-E-I-O.
With a **baa**, **baa**, here,
and a **baa**, **baa**, there,

here a **baa**, there a **baa**,
everywhere a **baa**, **baa**.

Old MacDonald had a farm, E-I-E-I-O!

And on that farm he had some hens, E-I-E-I-O!
With a *cluck*, *cluck*, here,
and a *cluck*, *cluck*, there,

here a cluck, there a *cluck*,
everyw a *cluck*, *cluck*.

Old MacDonald had a farm, E-I-E-I-O!

And on that farm he had some cows, *E-I-E-I-O!*
With a **moo**, **moo**, here,
and a **moo**, **moo**, there,

here a **moo**, there a **moo**,
everywhere a **moo**, **moo**.

Old MacDonald had a farm, E-I-E-I-O!

And on that farm he had some pigs, E-I-E-I-O!
With an **oink, oink,** here,
and an **oink, oink,** there,

here an **oink,** there an **oink,**
everywhere an **oink, oink.**

Old MacDonald had a farm, E-I-E-I-O!

Old MacDonald had a farm, E-I-E-I-O!

With a **moo, moo** here

and a **baa, baa** the[re]

an **oink, oink** here

and a *cluck, cluck* there

a **chug, chug** here

and a **woof, woof** there.

Old MacDonald had a farm, E-I-E-I-O!